ART HISTORY LESSONS

Children's Arts, Music & Photography Books

Speedy Publishing LLC
40 E. Main St. #1156
Newark, DE 19711
www.speedypublishing.com

Copyright © 2017

All Rights reserved. No part of this book may be reproduced or used in any way or form or by any means whether electronic or mechanical, this means that you cannot record or photocopy any material ideas or tips that are provided in this book.

In this book, we're going to talk about Pop Art and Abstract Art. So, let's get right to it!

Blonde Woman Thinking (pop art)

In the late 1950s, a new form of art emerged in the United Kingdom. It was called Pop Art. The Pop Art scene thrived in the 1960s and is still popular today. Just like many other cultural changes in the 1960s, it was designed to be "counterculture." This simply means that it broke the rules for what art was thought to be at the time.

Pop art Pow! Quote type poster banner.

For example, Pop Art challenged the serious subjects of the Renaissance and other styles of classical art by the use of its subject matter. It even challenged the seriousness of Abstract Art. Instead of using religious subjects, portraits, battle scenes, landscapes, or mythology for its subjects, it used common everyday items, such as soup cans with brand labels, popular soft drinks, faces of celebrities, colorful comic strips, and cartoon characters.

Andy Warhol: Campbell's Soup Cans (1962).

Pop Art poked fun of the serious tone of the art world and sent the message that art can be made from anything.

An earlier style of art called Dadaism, which was popular from 1916 through 1923, was the inspiration for Pop Art. It made fun of the art establishment by using everyday street images as well as commercial images for its subject matter.

What are the characteristics of Pop Art?

Pop Art is quirky. It uses bright, offbeat colors. It's composed of lots of repeated simple shapes. Bold outlines are favored over thin ones. Collages of different images or the same image are common. Colors and textures are changed within repeated images.

Set coffee mug artwork, pop art style.

The art is designed to make light of classical art, and is filled with humor, criticism of what is normally thought of as culture, and irony.

Portrait of Andy Warhol

Famous Artists of the Pop Art Movement

There were many famous artists during the Pop Art movement. Some of the most famous were:

Andy Warhol

Warhol is the best known of all the artists in the Pop Art Movement. He was influential in making Pop Art known throughout the world. In addition to painting everyday objects such as cans of Campbell's Soup in unique ways, Warhol frequently painted well-known celebrities, such as Elvis Presley, Elizabeth Taylor, and Marilyn Monroe.

JASPER JOHNS

Jasper Johns used iconic American images for some of his paintings, such as the flag and a map of the United States. Another famous painting by Johns has a pattern of numbers boxed out with splotchy vivid colors and yet another shows a colorful image of a target.

Jasper Johns, Target with Four Faces, 1955

Roy Lichtenstein

ROY LICHTENSTEIN

Lichtenstein was fascinated by the art in comic books and based his paintings on a comic book style. He even mimicked the dot patterns used to print comics in his paintings. He made his manmade art look as if it had been made by machine.

DAVID HOCKNEY

Hockney is known for Los Angeles suburban landscapes with swimming pools painted in vivid colors.

Hockney depicted in "The Threads That Bind Us", embroidered hanging, by Morwenna Catt and Lucas Stephens

Portrait of Wayne Thiebaud

WAYNE THIEBAUD

Thiebaud is known for his brightly colored paintings of diner and cafeteria food, such as pies, ice cream cones, and hotdogs. One of his most famous paintings is called "Three Machines" and depicts three old-fashioned gumball machines with colorful gumballs. Thiebaud's art has more warmth and playfulness than other works by Pop Artists.

KEITH HARING

Haring's art is well known for his cartoon-like, boldly outlined stick figures doing different things. His art has a look similar to street art or graffiti.

Keith Haring at work in the Stedelijk Museum in Amsterdam.

FAMOUS EXAMPLES OF POP ART

Pop art collage.

Marilyn Diptych by Andy Warhol

A diptych is a painting in two panels. Medieval paintings were created like this for religious figures, so Warhol seems to be saying that Marilyn is an icon to be worshipped. Warhol created this painting during the weeks directly after Marilyn Monroe's death in 1962. It shows fifty images of Marilyn's face.

Famous Marilyn Monroe picture from Andy Warhol.

Andy Warhol - Marilyn 1967.

It's the same image from a publicity still photo from one of her famous movies called Niagara. The twenty-five images on the left are in different bright colors, but the ones are the right are in black and white and leave you with a feeling of Marilyn's rise to fame and untimely death. This famous painting is housed in the Tate Modern in London.

WHAAM! BY ROY LICHTENSTEIN

This painting is also a diptych. On the left, a rocket blazes through the sky and we see the pilot's thoughts written in a thought bubble. On the right, there's an explosion with a big **"WHAAM!"** written in letters. The painting was based on an image from a comic book.

Roy Lichtenstein's Whaam! (1963) at Tate Modern

Three Flags by Jasper Johns

THREE FLAGS BY JASPER JOHNS

Johns had a dream about painting flags before he started to use them as a frequent form of subject matter. In this painting, he shows the viewer three images of the American flag, overlapped on top of each other with the largest one in back and the smallest one in front. The surface of the painting looks like a sculpture.

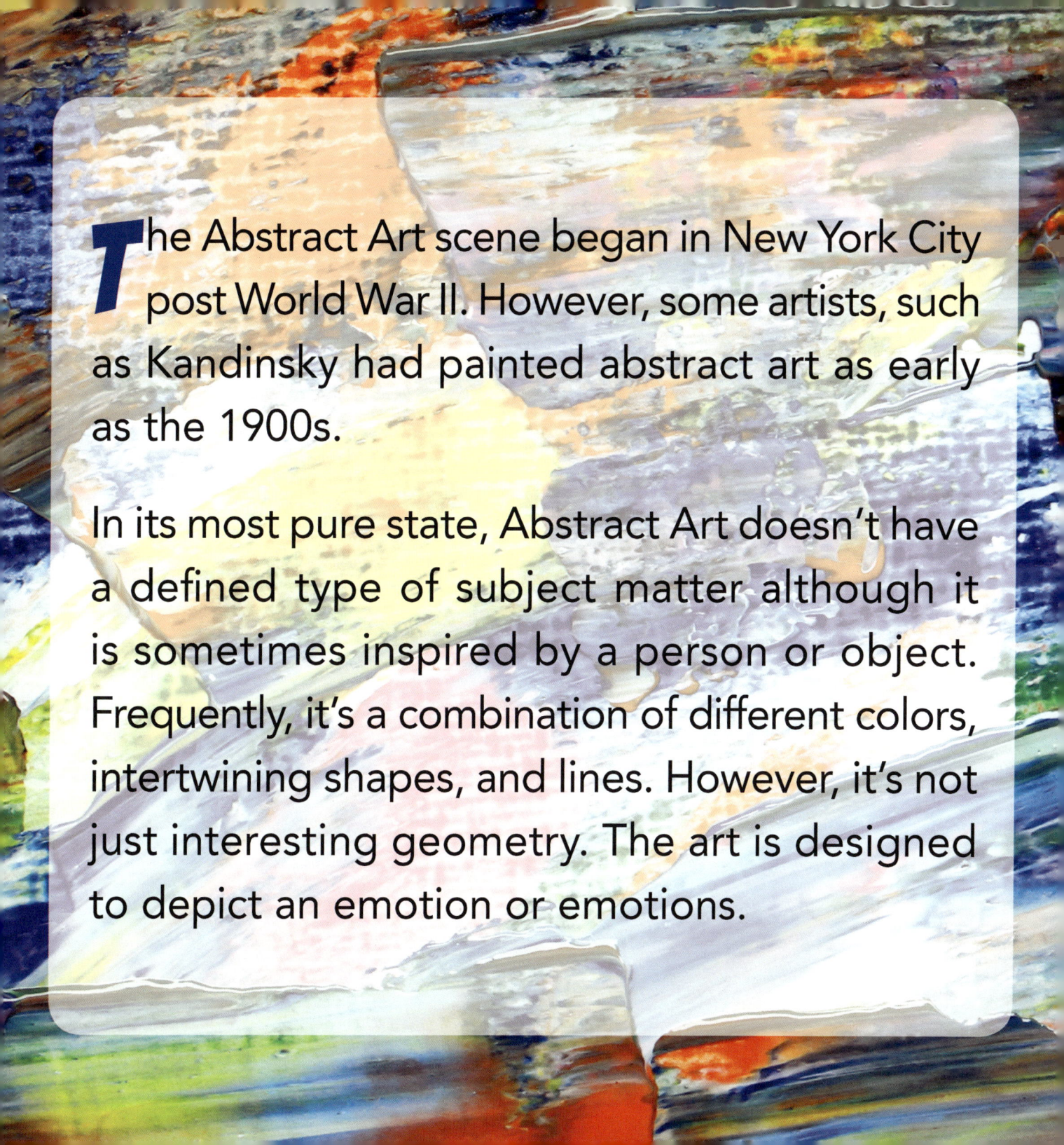

The Abstract Art scene began in New York City post World War II. However, some artists, such as Kandinsky had painted abstract art as early as the 1900s.

In its most pure state, Abstract Art doesn't have a defined type of subject matter although it is sometimes inspired by a person or object. Frequently, it's a combination of different colors, intertwining shapes, and lines. However, it's not just interesting geometry. The art is designed to depict an emotion or emotions.

WHAT ARE THE CHARACTERISTICS OF ABSTRACT ART?

Abstract Art doesn't always have a subject that can be recognized. Some artists working in this style had theories about which colors provoke which emotions. However, not all artists shared the same beliefs regarding color. Some artists planned out their paintings in vast detail before they began painting, while others just painted their own emotions in a seemingly random way, hoping that the viewers would be able to detect

Closeup of brush on palette.

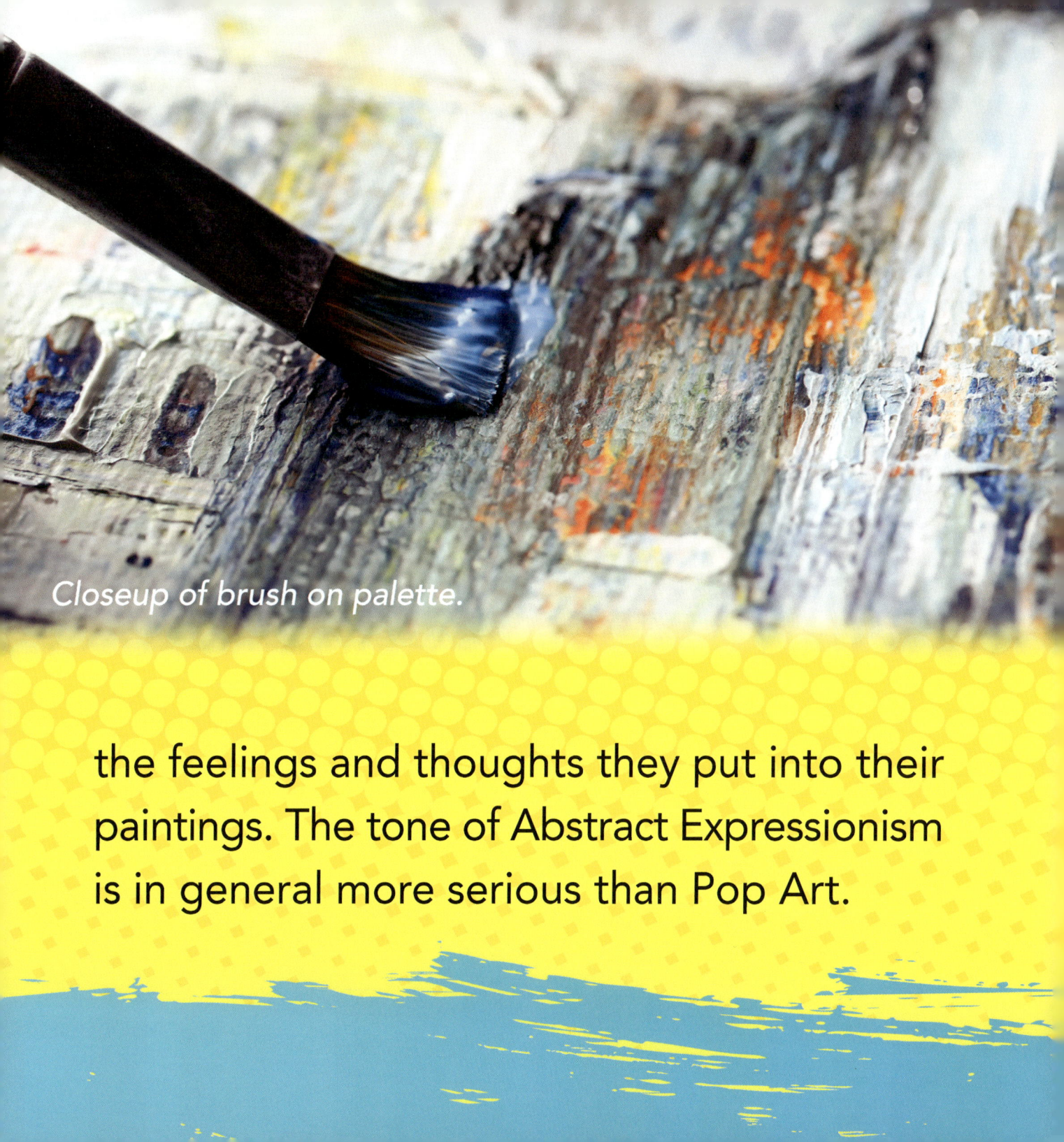

the feelings and thoughts they put into their paintings. The tone of Abstract Expressionism is in general more serious than Pop Art.

Famous Artists of the Abstract Expressionist Movement

There were many famous artists during this movement. Some of the most famous were:

Wassily Kandinsky

Kandinsky sought to put sounds as well as emotions into art. He's considered to be the first true painter of Abstract Art.

Wassily Kandinsky.

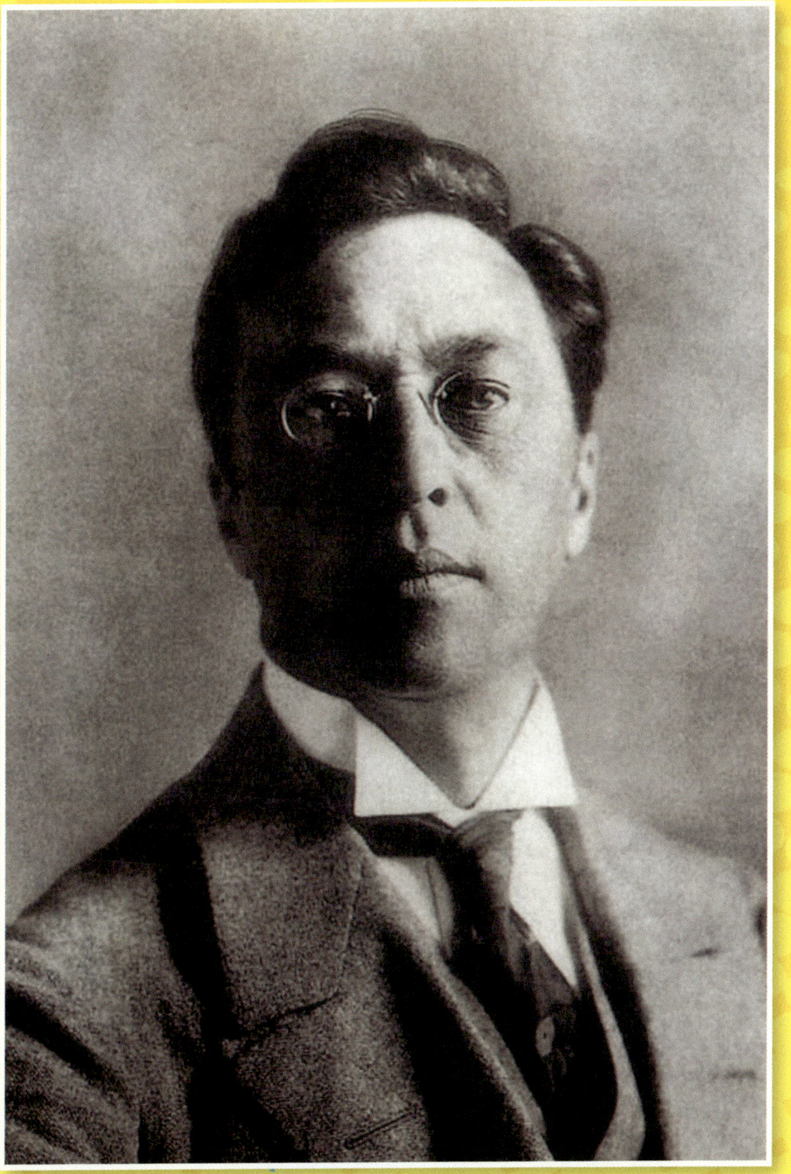

Mahoning (1956) by Franz Kline

FRANZ KLINE

Considered an Action Painter, Kline is known for his bold paintings with huge swashes of black against white. He felt the white areas were just as important as the black.

WILLEM DE KOONING

A Dutch artist, Kooning became part of the New York City movement of Abstract Expressionism. Woman III, one of his well-known paintings with tones of yellow and orange and swirling brush strokes in black, eventually sold for $137.5 million to billionaire investor Steven A. Cohen.

Willem de Kooning (1968).

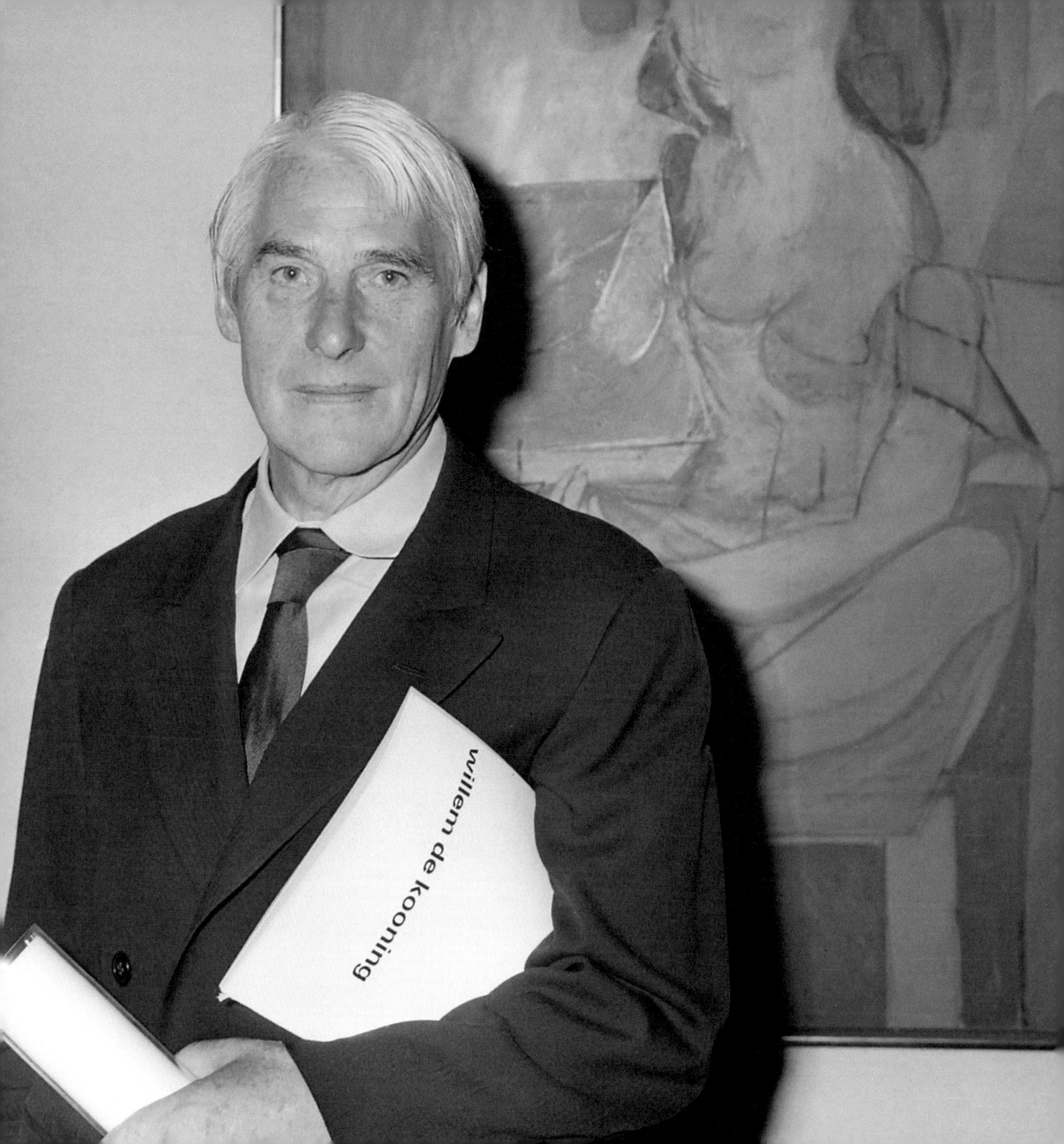
willem de kooning

Portrait of Piet Mondrian

PIET MONDRIAN

Mondrian's art technique, which he called *"The Style,"* was a precise geometric layout of flat color rectangles divided by straight lines. His paintings had a modern, clean look with primary colors set against white backgrounds with bold black lines.

JACKSON POLLOCK

Perhaps the most famous painter of this era, Pollock dripped and splashed paint on his canvases instead of using brush strokes. This style of painting was later called *"action painting."*

MARK ROTHKO

Rothko's paintings have huge blocks of intense color with edges that blend softly together. Some blocks are wide and tall and others are wide and short.

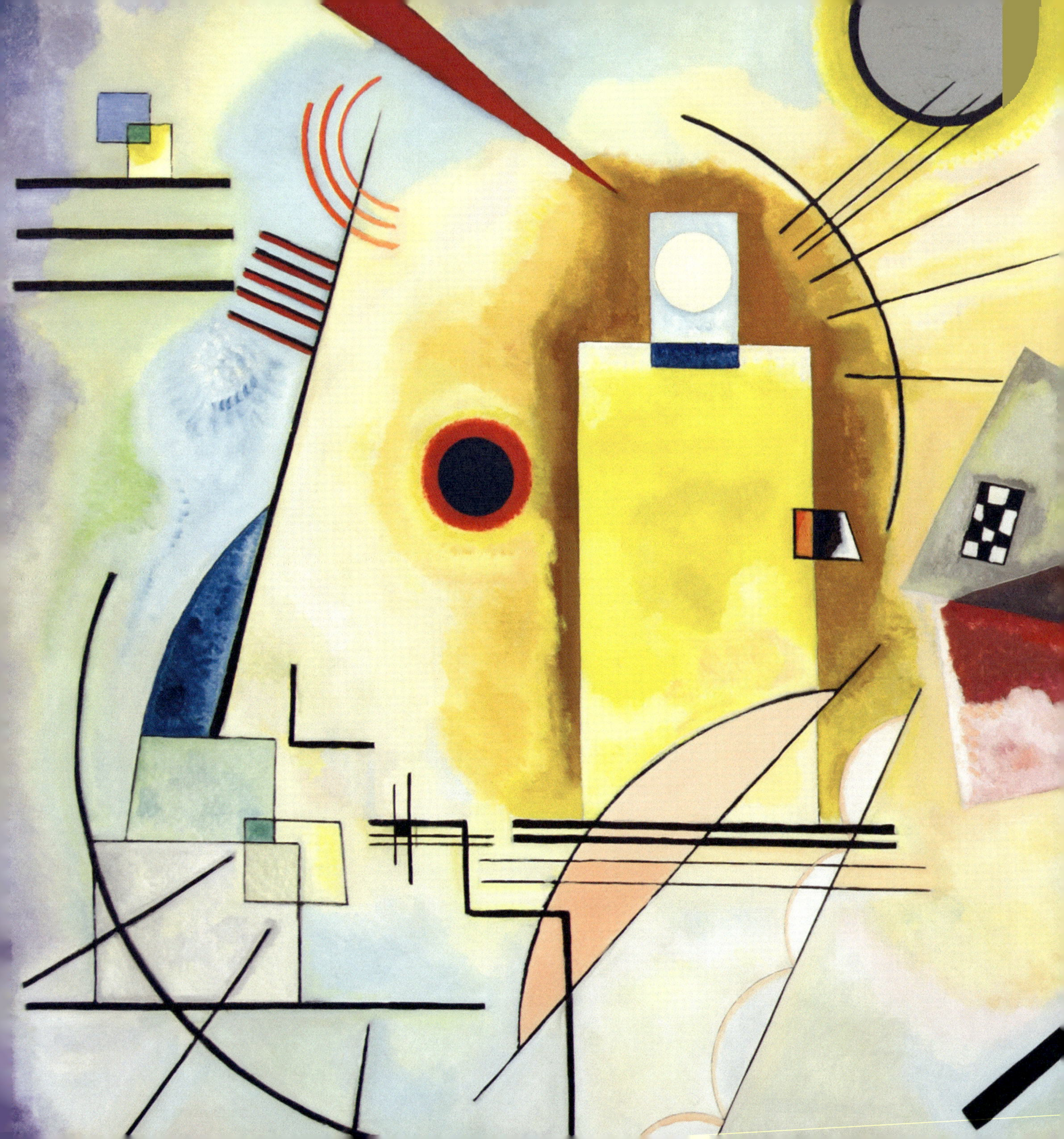

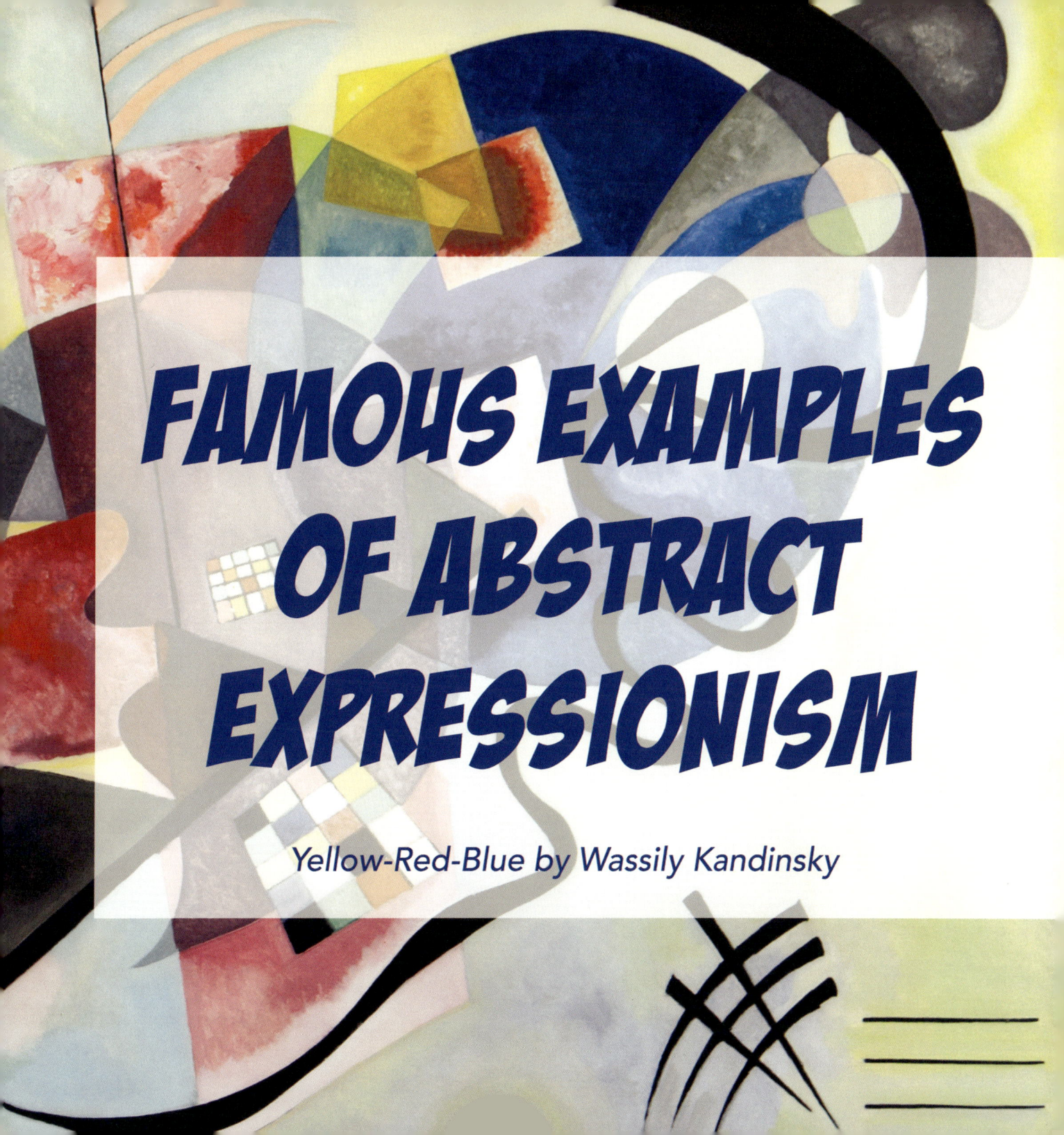

Famous Examples of Abstract Expressionism

Yellow-Red-Blue by Wassily Kandinsky

White Center by Mark Rothko

This painting is a vertically oriented rectangle and represents Rothko's signature style. On a rose-colored background that varies in color intensity, there is a yellow horizontal rectangle, a thin black strip that borders it at the bottom, then a white center followed by a pink rectangular shape. The swatches of color have soft edges. It's not clear what emotion the painting is supposed to represent.

White Center (Yellow, Pink and Lavender on Rose) by Rothko.

The artist has left it to the viewer to interpret the painting's meaning. In 2006, this masterpiece of abstract expressionism sold for $72 million.

No. 5, 1948 by Jackson Pollock

Pollock's style of painting was unique to him. He would drop or splash the paint directly onto the canvas. In this masterpiece, brown paint and yellow paint are painted on top of each other in a dizzying area of lines, blended colors, and unique textures. In 2006, this Pollock painting sold for $140 million.

No. 5, 1948 by Pollock

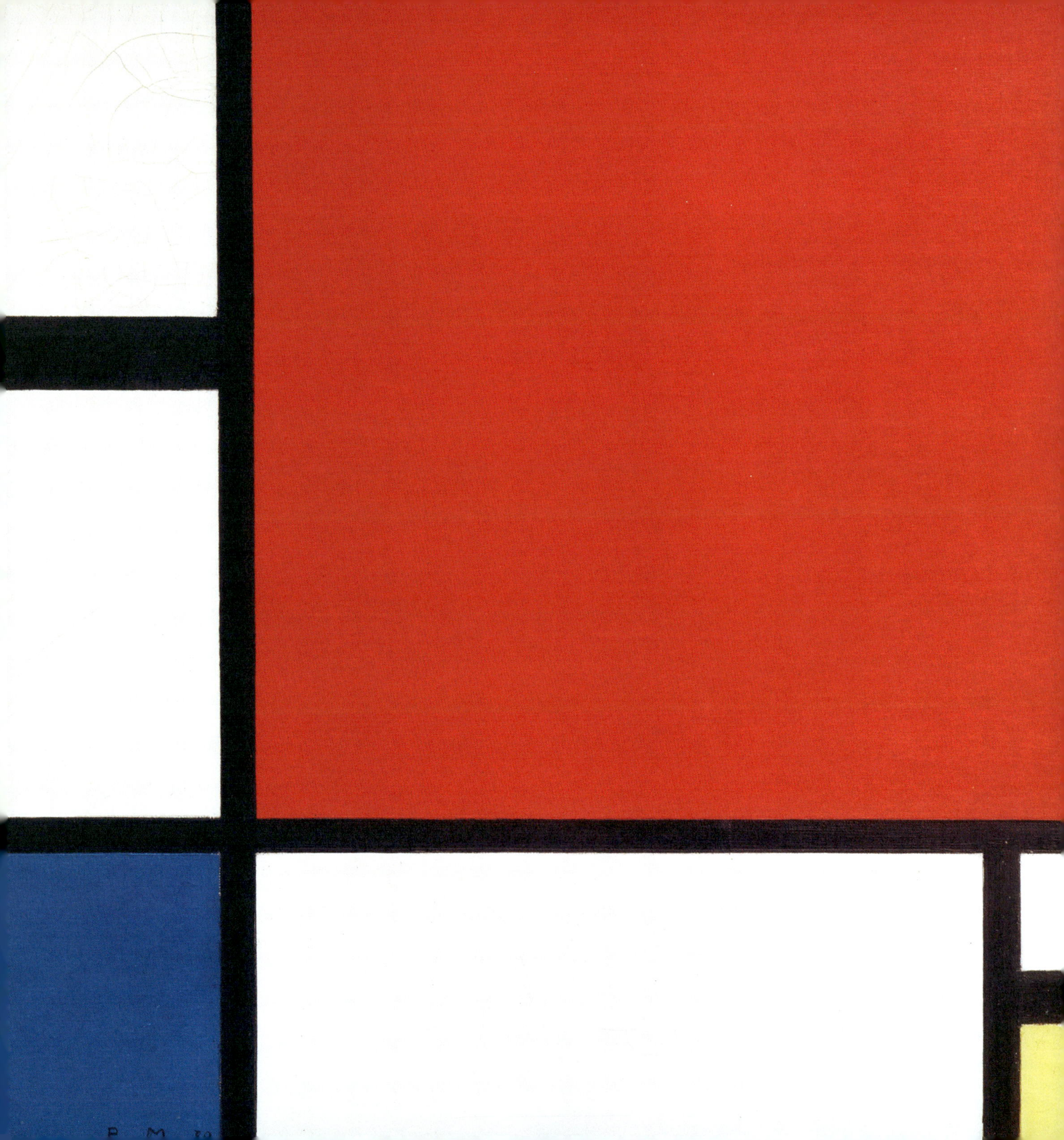

COMPOSITION II BY PIET MONDRIAN

An array of primary colors boxed in with a white background and precise black lines, this painting is an example of *"The Style"* that Mondrian became famous for.

Mondrian's Composition II in Red, Blue, and Yellow.

POP ART COMPARED TO ABSTRACT ART

Both Pop Art and Abstract Art are two modern forms of art, but they differ greatly in their approach. Pop Art pokes fun at the seriousness of art. In many cases it takes its inspiration from something that already exists in some form, like a photograph of a celebrity or a common household item. Abstract Art uses more fine art techniques for a wide variety of subject matter, some of which is hard to define.

Gaping girl pop art style.

Abstract Art is a more serious art form than Pop Art. Both forms of art strive to evoke a specific emotion in the viewer from fear to joy and everything in between.

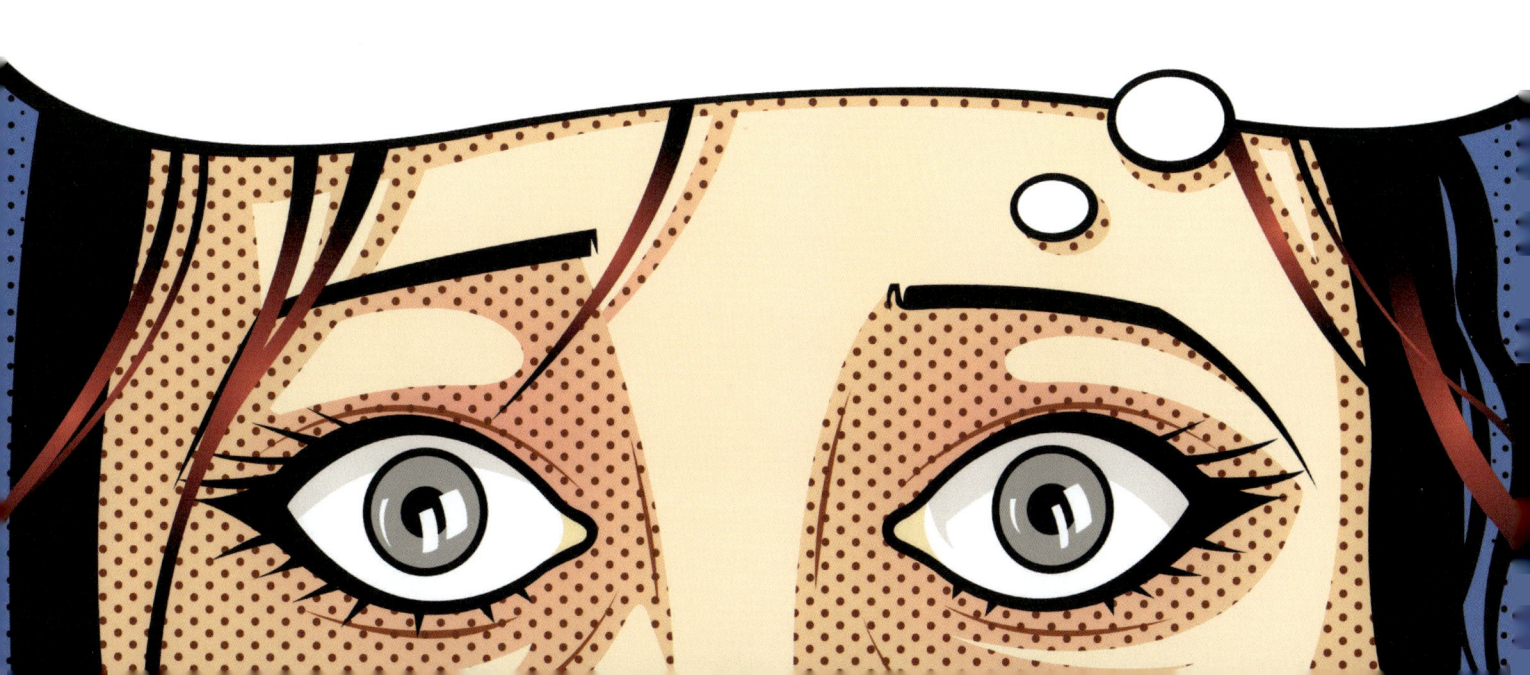

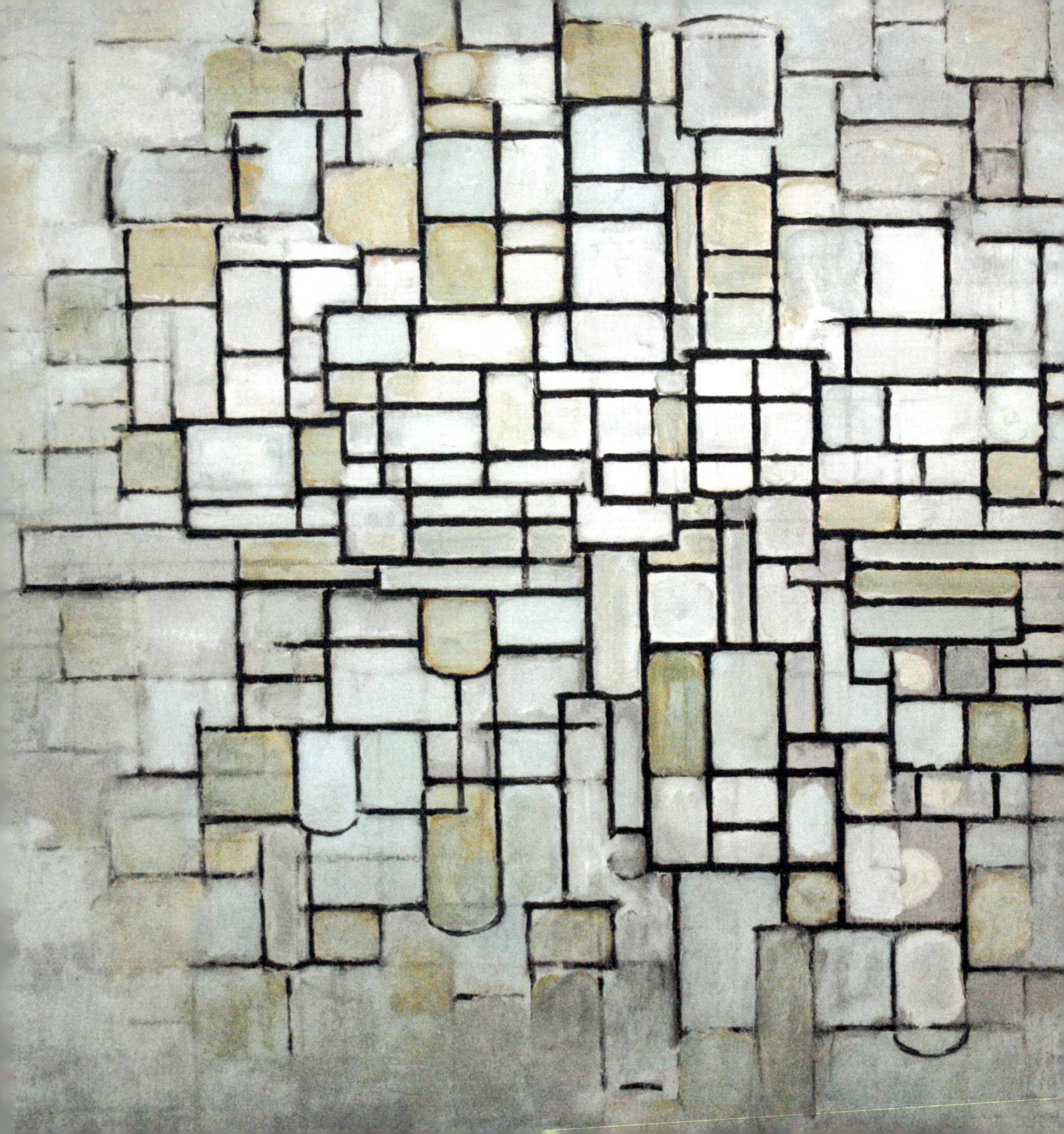

Awesome! Now you know more about the unique styles of Pop Art and Abstract Art. You can find more Art, Music, and Photography books from Baby Professor by searching the website of your favorite book retailer.

Composition No. 11 by Mondrian.

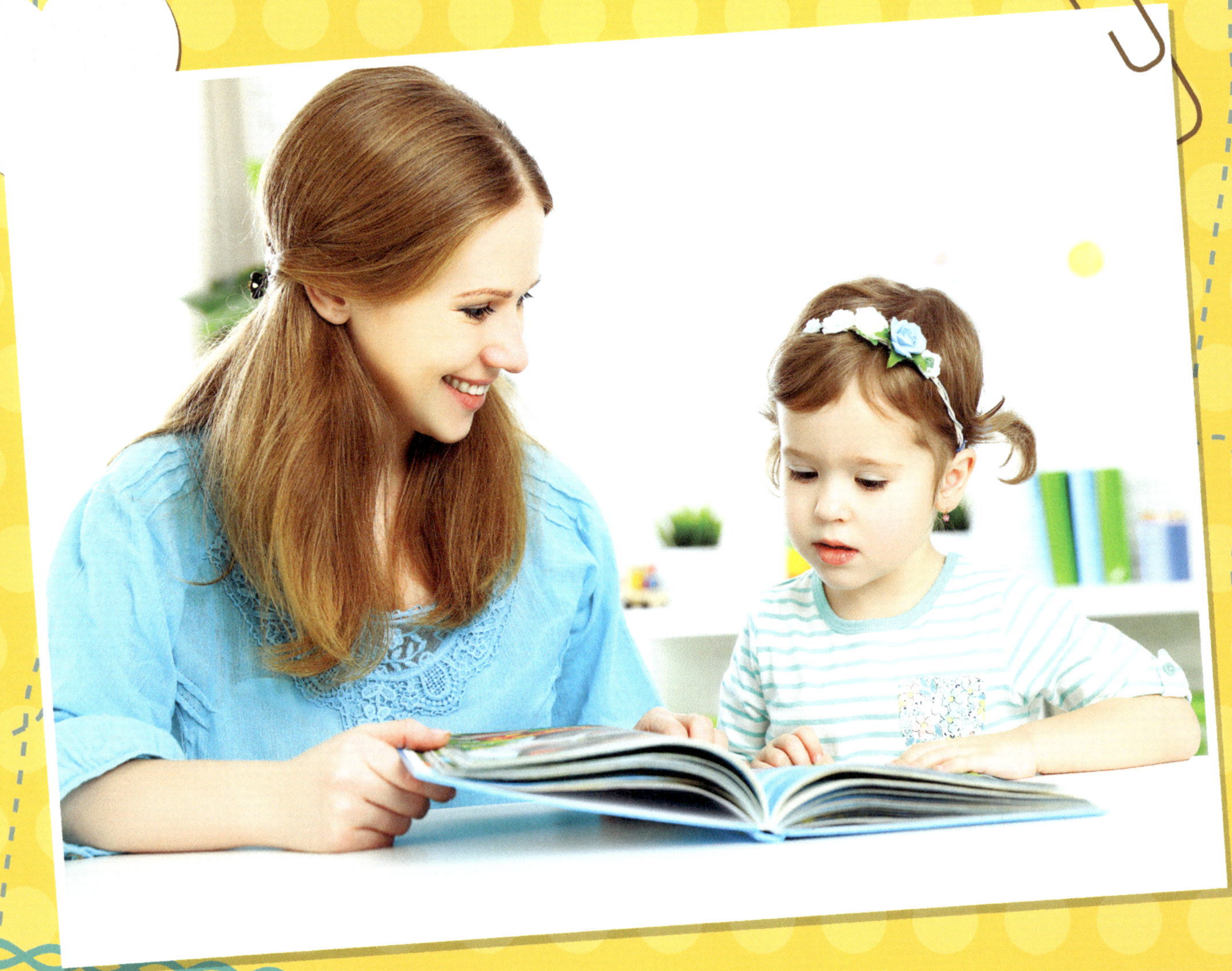

Visit

BABY PROFESSOR
EDUCATION KIDS

www.BabyProfessorBooks.com

to download Free Baby Professor eBooks and view our catalog of new and exciting Children's Books

Printed in Great Britain
by Amazon